If you have a home computer with Internet access you may:
- request an item to be placed on hold.
- renew an item that is not overdue or on hold.
- view titles and due dates checked out on your card.
- view and/or pay your outstanding fines online ($1 & over).

To view your patron record from your home computer click on Patchogue-Medford Library's homepage: www.pmlib.org

Haunted Caves

by Natalie Lunis

Consultant: Troy Taylor
President of the American Ghost Society

BEARPORT
PUBLISHING

New York, New York

Credits

Cover and Title Page, © Stephen G. Page/Shutterstock and © Filip Fuxa/Shutterstock; 4–5, © andreiuc88/Shutterstock; 6, © Jim Ambs/Kentuckytravels.blogspot.com; 7, © Jim Ambs/Kentuckytravels.blogspot.com; 8, © Ed Prescott; 9TR, © Chuck Franklin/Alamy; 9CR, © David L. Moore/OR10/Alamy; 9B, © Richard Ondrovic/richardondrovic.com; 10, © Gary Burke; 11T, © Stocksnapper/Shutterstock; 11B, Title page illustration from original printing of "The Pennsylvania Hermit," ca. 1838; 12 © Courtesy of Marengo Cave, Indiana; 13, © Courtesy of Marengo Cave, Indiana; 14, © Caitlin Mirra/Shutterstock; 15, © NY Daily News Archive via Getty Images; 16, © Carol Von Canon; 17, © Carol Von Canon; 18, Courtesy of St. Louis Postcard; 19, © Enrico Pajello/Reuters/Landov; 20, © Roy Griffiths; 20–21, © Robert Stainforth/Alamy; 22, © Kumar Sriskandan/Alamy; 23, © Glenn Berg from Canada; 24–25, Kim Jones; 25L, © Kjetil Bjørnsrud; 25R, © Mercat Tours Ltd.; 26T, © Erik W. Grow/Shutterstock; 26B, © Paul Mison; 27L, © Corbis; 27R, © Patrick Schroff.

Publisher: Kenn Goin
Editorial Director: Adam Siegel
Creative Director: Spencer Brinker
Design: Dawn Beard Creative
Cover: Dawn Beard Creative and Kim Jones
Photo Researcher: Picture Perfect Professionals, LLC

Library of Congress Cataloging-in-Publication Data

Lunis, Natalie.
  Haunted caves / by Natalie Lunis.
     p. cm. — (Scary places)
  Includes bibliographical references and index.
  ISBN-13: 978-1-61772-456-5 (library binding)
  ISBN-10: 1-61772-456-4 (library binding)
  1. Caves—Juvenile literature. 2. Haunted places—Juvenile literature. I. Title.
  GB601.2.L86 2012
  133.10914'4—dc23
                          2011044447

For more information, write to Bearport Publishing Company, Inc., 45 West 21st Street, Suite 3B, New York, New York 10010. Printed in the United States of America in North Mankato, Minnesota.

10 9 8 7 6 5 4 3 2 1

Contents

Haunted Caves

Caves are scary places. They're deep, dark, and cold. They are even scarier, however, when they are haunted—as many of these tunnels into the ground are thought to be. In fact, some people say that caves are among the most ghostly places on Earth.

Why do caves attract so many ghosts? Some say that the underground spaces serve as passageways between the world of the living and the **spirit world**. Others believe that people who have lost their lives in the underground spaces are unable ever to leave the caves again. Whatever the reason, in the 11 haunted caves in this book you'll meet many of these ghosts. Among them are a man whose heart was broken because he could not save his sister's life, a doomed explorer who was trapped belowground, and a mysterious girl in a polka-dot dress. Do not **linger** with them too long, however. Sooner or later, you'll want to see the light of day again.

A Witchy Ghost

The Bell Witch Cave, Adams, Tennessee

The Bell Witch is one of America's most famous ghosts—and also one of the fiercest. This spirit once caused all kinds of trouble for a family living on a Tennessee farm. It wasn't long, however, until visitors to a nearby cave could also feel the witch's **fury**.

In the early 1800s, a **settler** named John Bell moved with his family to northern Tennessee. The Bells worked hard to build a house and start a farm. Then, in 1817, the horrible problems began.

The entrance to the Bell Witch Cave

Inside the house, the Bells heard knocking and scratching noises. Then bedsheets were pulled off sleeping children and guests. Family members were slapped and had their hair pulled by an unseen force. After a while, the ghost started talking, revealing to them that its name was Kate. People thought that the angry spirit must be a witch sent by Kate Batts, a neighbor who had once had an argument over money with John Bell.

In 1821, about a year after John's death, the spirit left the Bell home. She didn't go far, however. Since that time, her presence has often been felt in a nearby cave—now called the Bell Witch Cave. If the reports of visitors and guides are true, the witch still has a **temper**. She has been said to grab, pin down, and slap people who go on the underground tour—especially those who dare to express any doubts that she exists.

Inside the Bell Witch Cave

Once, a group of teenagers visited the Bell Witch Cave. After complaining that they hadn't seen any ghosts, one girl was pushed to the ground by an unseen force. She then felt a slap. When the tour guide shined a light on her face, everyone could see red marks— which looked like the prints of fingers.

A Ghost of the Civil War

Craighead Caverns, Sweetwater, Tennessee

Do some ghosts haunt caves because they are the places where their lives were lost? That may be true for one soldier. He is said to have remained in a Tennessee cave long after the war he was fighting in ended.

Inside Craighead Caverns

For a long time, a series of caves now known as Craighead **Caverns** served as shelter for Cherokee Indians. These first discoverers of the caves left behind a rich assortment of belongings, including arrowheads, jewelry, and pottery. Later, in the 1820s, the first white settlers in the area started using the caves in a different way. They stored potatoes and other foods inside the cool underground spaces.

Arrowheads made by Cherokees

During the **Civil War** (1861–1865), the caves served yet another purpose. Deep inside, **Confederate soldiers** dug for saltpeter, a rock salt that was needed to make gunpowder. According to a diary that one of the soldiers left behind, a spy from the enemy side discovered the **mine** and tried to blow it up. However, the **Union soldier** was captured and shot just outside the cave entrance before he could carry out his plan. Since that time, according to people who know the area well, his ghost has been spotted inside Craighead Caverns—one more piece of history that has been left behind in the deep, dark caves.

A Union soldier

The Lost Sea

The largest underground lake in the United States, known as the Lost Sea, lies deep within Craighead Caverns. The four-and-a-half-acre (1.8-hectare) lake was discovered by a 13-year-old boy in 1905—exactly 40 years after the Civil War ended.

The Pennsylvania Hermit

Indian Echo Caverns, Hummelstown, Pennsylvania

A story from Pennsylvania's history tells of a **hermit** who wandered the countryside and then lived the last 19 years of his life in a cave. Who was this man—and why would he choose to spend so much time in such a dark, lonely place?

Inside Indian
Echo Caverns

William Wilson and his younger sister Elizabeth were both born on a farm not far from Philadelphia in the 1760s. In 1785, at the age of 20 or so, Elizabeth was accused of murder, found guilty, and sentenced to hang. William, who was working as a stone carver in another town, heard about what had happened and worked hard to get her freed. He gathered evidence of Elizabeth's innocence and received a **pardon** for her. Tragically, however, he arrived at the **execution** just minutes too late. Elizabeth had already been hung.

William never got over his sister's death. He wandered through parts of Pennsylvania for 17 years and then reached a hilly area with many caves. He finally settled down in one of them and lived there all alone until his death in 1821. According to some versions of his story, even then he was unable to find peace. As a result, his ghost has haunted the cave ever since. According to others, however, two lonely spirits have been spotted wandering the caverns. Could they be brother and sister, reunited at last?

William Wilson, the Pennsylvania hermit

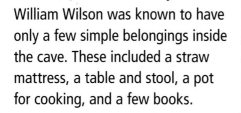

William Wilson was known to have only a few simple belongings inside the cave. These included a straw mattress, a table and stool, a pot for cooking, and a few books.

The Guide Who Wouldn't Leave

Marengo Cave, Marengo, Indiana

Caves aren't always creepy and scary—they can also be beautiful. That's what people living in Marengo, Indiana, found out after two children discovered a huge cave just outside town. It's also how a man named Bill Clifton felt. He loved the cave so much that he found it hard to stay away—even after his death.

Marengo Cave

One September day in 1883, 15-year-old Blanche Hiestand and her younger brother Orris went out exploring. They made their way down an opening in the ground and were stunned by what they found. The opening led to a huge underground **chamber** filled with shimmering **rock formations**.

The owner of the property, sure that people would pay to see these underground wonders, soon started offering tours of the cave. By far, the most **dedicated** guide ever to lead the tours was a man named Bill Clifton. For more than 50 years, Clifton took visitors through Marengo Cave no matter how early or late in the day they arrived. When he **retired** in 1965 at the age of 79, he continued to live nearby.

After Bill's death in 1980, people who entered the caves started noticing strange things. One guide heard the entrance door slam shut—even though no one had come in. People on tours have heard both singing and rhythmic tapping. Are there natural explanations for these happenings? Or are they signs that Bill Clifton never left the cave he knew and loved so well?

Inside Marengo Cave

During the time the cave has been open to the public, weddings, dances, and theater performances have taken place inside. At one wedding, Bill Clifton provided music by tapping on different parts of the cave with a wooden hammer.

Trapped Forever?

Mammoth Cave, Mammoth Cave National Park, Kentucky

Floyd Collins was born near Mammoth Cave, the largest **cave system** in the world. While he was growing up in the early 1900s, several sections were famous as show caves, where tickets were sold and tours were offered. Floyd badly wanted to find new underground areas that would bring in money for his family. Unfortunately, he ended up paying a huge price for trying to make such a discovery.

Inside part of the Mammoth Cave system

In 1917, Floyd Collins discovered a new part of the Mammoth system, which became a show cave known as Crystal Cave. In 1925, eager for more discoveries, he started exploring a small passageway known as Sand Cave. While crawling through a narrow area on his belly, he loosened a large heavy rock. It pinned his ankle so that he could not move any farther. Rescue crews found him, but because of the narrowness of the spot, no one could reach him. After being trapped underground for about 15 days, Floyd Collins died.

In the years following the deadly accident, stories about Floyd's ghost began to appear. An especially chilling one traces back to 1976, when two workers were checking water levels near Sand Cave. One of them heard the voice of a man, but it was not that of his partner. The voice called out, "Help me! Help me, I'm trapped! Johnny, help me!" Oddly, the last person Floyd Collins had spoken to before becoming trapped was a friend—whose name was Johnny Gerald.

The attempt to rescue Floyd Collins became a huge news story. Reporters from all over the country camped out near the entrance to Sand Cave. One newspaper writer named Skeets Miller even crawled into the cave several times to interview the trapped man.

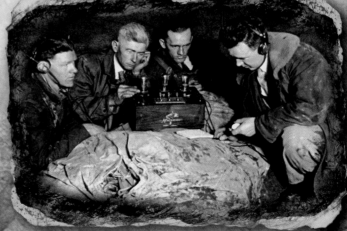

Outside the cave, people used special instruments to try to hear whether Floyd Collins's heart was still beating.

Send In the Ghost Hunters

Fantastic Caverns, Springfield, Missouri

Many ghosts have well-known histories. Some, however, are more mysterious. When a spirit's identity is unknown, ghost hunters are sometimes called in. That's what happened in one Missouri cave, where a girl in a polka-dot dress has appeared—for reasons no one can explain.

Inside Fantastic Caverns

In 1862, a Missouri farmer named John Knox went out hunting with his dog. Together, the two discovered the entrance to a deep set of caverns. A few years later, John placed an ad in a newspaper inviting volunteers to explore the cave. Twelve women from the Springfield Women's Athletic Club stepped forward as a result. They arrived with ropes and ladders and entered the caves. Once there, they carved their initials into the rock, leaving a reminder of their visit.

During the 1950s, the cave was named Fantastic Caverns and opened for tours. Since that time, many strange sights have been reported, including a ghostly girl in a polka-dot dress.

To learn more about the possible haunting, the cave's owners allowed ghost hunters—people who track down spirits—to investigate the caves. So far, however, the case is still unsolved. The experts have not been able to figure out who the girl in the polka-dot dress is—or rather who she *was*.

People have found strange glowing shapes in photos they have taken while visiting Fantastic Caverns. Ghost hunters call these shapes orbs. Orbs often appear in photos taken in places that are thought to be haunted.

Fantastic Caverns

A Cave with a Curse

English Cave, Saint Louis, Missouri

The city of Saint Louis is built over a huge, web-like system of natural caves. Today, most of them are filled up with water and forgotten. English Cave, however, is well known to many people. When they talk about the cave's past, they are likely to say that it is not only haunted but **cursed** as well.

Today, English Cave is completely flooded. It lies beneath Benton Park in Saint Louis, which is shown here.

Like many caves in the United States, English Cave was first discovered and used by **Native Americans**. According to **legend**, the cave also came to be haunted by the spirits of two Native Americans—a young man and young woman who died there.

The couple fell in love but had to run away and hide in the cave because the tribe's chief wanted to marry the woman himself. He was determined to capture the young people and waited outside the cave with a group of warriors. Refusing to be taken back, the couple stayed inside and starved to death.

In later years, several people bought the land and tried to use the cave for different businesses. In the 1840s, Ezra English—for whom the cave is named—opened an underground restaurant and music hall. In 1887, another owner started a mushroom farm. In 1897, yet another owner used the cave as storage space for his nearby **winery**. Each of the businesses failed after a short time, however. Did the terrible events of long ago cause all the bad luck? People in Saint Louis sometimes ask themselves that question.

No one knows whether the story of the young Native American man and woman dying in English Cave is true. However, it is known that the first white explorers who entered the cave found the bones of two people inside.

19

The Stolen Heart

Hell-Fire Caves, West Wycombe, England

Many caves were carved out by natural forces, such as flowing water from rivers. Some, however, were dug out of the earth by people for purposes such as **mining** or providing shelter or a hiding place. One famous set of caves was even created to serve as a meeting place for English gentlemen. These human-made spaces may not be as old as caves carved out by nature, but they can be just as haunted.

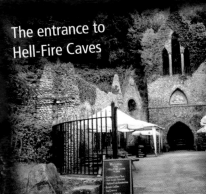

The entrance to Hell-Fire Caves

The Hell-Fire Caves were named after the Hell-Fire Club—a group that met there during the mid-1700s. The founder of the club, Sir Francis Dashwood, hired local workers to dig a series of underground rooms out of a hill near his family's home. He then invited his closest friends—who happened to be some of the richest and most powerful men in England—to join him for meetings and fancy dinners in the cave's elegantly decorated chambers.

Some people say that one of the members of the club, Paul Whitehead, never left the caves. When he died in 1774, Whitehead left some money to Sir Francis. The money was to be used to buy an **urn**—in which Whitehead's heart was to be kept, always at his beloved club. Sir Francis honored his friend's wishes. Unfortunately, during the 1820s, someone stole the heart. The urn, however, was left behind and kept in the caves, where it can still be seen by visitors. According to some, so can Whitehead's ghost—perhaps forever searching for his lost heart.

Inside the
Hell-Fire Caves

The caves have been open to visitors since 1951. More than two million people have toured them.

A Deep, Dark Shelter

Chislehurst Caves, Bromley, England

Thousands of years ago, before people started building towns and cities, early humans in some parts of the world used caves for shelter. Surprisingly, in modern times, people have also found **refuge** in these spaces carved out of the earth.

A tour group entering
Chislehurst Caves

Chislehurst Caves were not formed by nature, but they are older than many other human-made caves. The history of the caves, which are just outside London, goes back about 5,000 years. The people who created and worked inside the caves used them for mining both flint, a hard rock used to make tools and simple weapons, and chalk, a soft rock used to make plaster.

During **World War II** (1939–1945), English men, women, and children living near the caves moved into them to escape the bombs being dropped by German planes. At one point, 15,000 people were using the huge **air raid shelter**, sleeping in bunk beds that had been built for this special purpose. There were even two churches and a hospital set up within the caves.

Nowadays, the caves are open for tours, as well as for parties. During these events, however, tourists and partygoers sometimes hear strange noises—most often footsteps or the voices of children. Are these the sounds of spirits, reminding today's visitors of the caves' long and unusual history?

During the tour of Chislehurst Caves, visitors see **mannequins** dressed and posed to show how people who used the caves during World War II would have looked.

Life—and Death—Underground

The South Bridge Vaults, Edinburgh, Scotland

Edinburgh, Scotland, is said to be one of the most haunted cities in the world. So it's not hard to imagine how chilling one of the city's most haunted places is—especially since it is a cluster of human-made caves that are part of a huge stone bridge.

In the late 1700s, space was hard to find in the busy city of Edinburgh. As a result, people put up buildings on top of South Bridge, a huge stone structure featuring 19 openings, or arches. The arches—which had now become underground spaces—were also put to use. Business owners put in floors and ceilings to create many small rooms, known as **vaults**, which could be used for storage and as workshops.

buildings

vaults   South Bridge

After only a few years, the vaults were abandoned because water was seeping in, resulting in floods. At that point, the city's poorest residents moved in, making homes out of the cold, damp, dark spaces. Crime, disease, and death were common in the cramped **urban** caves, and after 50 years or so, the vaults were once again abandoned.

The South Bridge Vaults were forgotten until the 1980s, when they were rediscovered and soon opened for tours. Not surprisingly, there have since been many reports of ghostly activities in this place that was once so dirty, dangerous, and deadly. Among the vaults' most famous ghosts is a boy known as Jack, who is reported to grab the hands of unsuspecting visitors.

One of the vaults

Inside the vaults

Several of the ghosts who are said to haunt the South Bridge Vaults have become well known in Edinburgh, including an angry spirit named Mr. Boots. People claim he pushes visitors and throws rocks at them.

Washed Away

Sutro Baths, San Francisco, California

For more than 60 years, the Sutro Baths were a major attraction in San Francisco, welcoming thousands of swimmers at a time. Today, in the **ruins** that remain, a sign warns visitors of the danger of drowning. Does it also provide a hint about why a human-made cave at the site might be haunted?

The ruins of the Sutro Baths

CAUTION

CLIFF AND SURF AREA
EXTREMELY DANGEROUS
People have been swept
from the rocks and drowned

The warning sign

When they opened in 1896, the Sutro Baths were anything but dark and scary. This stunning set of indoor swimming pools was located on the coastline of the Pacific Ocean. The building that enclosed them contained 100,000 square feet (9,290 sq m) of glass, letting in lots of natural light.

During the 1960s, however, the baths were closed down. As the giant structure was being demolished, a fire broke out. Only ruins were left behind.

Because of the **rugged** and beautiful setting of the baths, many people come to explore the crumbling remains. Most of them stop to read a sign that warns them to be careful, explaining that "people have been swept from the rocks and drowned." Only the bravest of these visitors dare to enter a human-made cave by the sea, where the crashing waves are especially loud. Why? It is said that the cave is haunted by the souls of people who were washed away and drowned in the rough waters—just as the sign says.

The Sutro Baths around the early 1900s

The human-made cave that is said to be haunted was dug out to provide rock for building the baths.

Haunted Caves

Marengo Cave
Marengo, Indiana

A cave so beautiful that a longtime tour guide cannot bring himself to leave

Sutro Baths
San Francisco, California

Do drowning victims haunt this cave?

Fantastic Caverns
Springfield, Missouri

A girl in a polka-dot dress whose presence no one can explain

English Cave
Saint Louis, Missouri

A cave that might be cursed because of two people in love who died there

The Bell Witch Cave
Adams, Tennessee

A witch-like ghost attacks visitors.

Craighead Caverns
Sweetwater, Tennessee

A soldier who never returned from the Civil War may still haunt this underground mine.

Indian Echo Caverns
Hummelstown, Pennsylvania

A home to a hermit who could not save his sister

Mammoth Cave
Mammoth Cave National Park, Kentucky

A cave explorer is trapped—perhaps forever.

NORTH AMERICA

SOUTH AMERICA

Atlantic Ocean

Pacific Ocean

Around the World

Arctic
Ocean

EUROPE

ASIA

AFRICA

The South Bridge Vaults
Edinburgh, Scotland

Long ago, the city's poorest
lived—and died—here.

Hell-Fire Caves
West Wycombe, England

An English gentleman searches
for his stolen heart.

Chislehurst Caves
Bromley, England

During World War II, thousands
of people found shelter here.
Did some never leave?

Indian
Ocean

AUSTRALIA

N
W E
S

Southern
Ocean

ANTARCTICA

Glossary

air raid shelter (AIR RAYD SHEL-tur) a place people go to find safety during a bombing from the air

caverns (KAV-urnz) another word for *caves*

cave system (KAYV SISS-tuhm) a set of connected caves

chamber (CHAYM-bur) a closed-in space

Civil War (SIV-il WOR) The U.S. war between the Southern states and the Northern states, which lasted from 1861 to 1865

Confederate soldiers (*kuhn*-FED-ur-uht SOHL-jurz) people who fought for the Southern states during the U.S. Civil War

cursed (KURST) under an evil spell and therefore likely to cause unhappiness

dedicated (DED-uh-*kayt*-id) loyal

execution (eks-uh-KYOO-shuhn) punishment by death

fury (FYOOR-ee) anger

hermit (HUR-mit) a person who lives alone and hides away from the rest of the world

legend (LEJ-uhnd) a story that has been passed down from long ago that may be based on fact but is not always completely true

linger (LING-ur) to stay longer than expected

mannequins (MAN-uh-kinz) life-size dummies

mine (MYEN) a deep hole or tunnel from which rock or other materials are taken

mining (MYE-ning) the digging of deep holes or tunnels from which rock or other materials are taken

Native Americans (NAY-tiv uh-MER-uh-kinz) the first people to live in America; they are sometimes called American Indians

pardon (PAR-duhn) release from punishment

refuge (REF-yooj) safety and protection

retired (ri-TYERD) stopped working

rock formations (ROK for-MAY-shuhnz) rocks that have special shapes

rugged (RUHG-id) having a surface that is rough and uneven

ruins (ROO-inz) what is left of something that has collapsed or been destroyed

settler (SET-lur) a person who makes a home in a new place

spirit world (SPIHR-it WURLD) the world of supernatural creatures, such as ghosts

temper (TEM-pur) a tendency to get angry

Union soldier (YOON-yuhn SOHL-jur) a person who fought for the Northern states during the U.S. Civil War

urban (UR-buhn) having to do with cities

urn (URN) a large vase with a base

vaults (VAWLTS) places, sometimes dug into the ground, for keeping or protecting things

winery (WYE-nur-ee) a place where wine is made

World War II (WURLD WOR TOO) a worldwide conflict that involved many countries and lasted from 1939 to 1945

Bibliography

Austin, Joanne. *Weird Hauntings: True Tales of Ghostly Places.* New York: Sterling (2006).

Hauck, Dennis William. *The International Directory of Haunted Places.* New York: Penguin Books (2000).

Lankford, Andrea. *Haunted Hikes: Spine-Tingling Tales and Trails from North America's National Parks.* Santa Monica, CA: Santa Monica Press (2006).

Taylor, Troy. *Down in the Darkness: The Shadowy History of America's Haunted Mines, Tunnels & Caverns.* Alton, IL: Whitechapel Press (2003).

Read More

Banks, Cameron. *America's Most Haunted.* New York: Scholastic (2002).

Goodman, Michael, E. *Dark Labyrinths (Scary Places).* New York: Bearport (2010).

Hamilton, John. *Haunted Places (The World of Horror).* Edina, MN: ABDO (2007).

Parvis, Sarah. *Ghost Towns (Scary Places).* New York: Bearport (2008).

Williams, Dinah. *Haunted Houses (Scary Places).* New York: Bearport (2008).

Williams, Dinah. *Spooky Cemeteries (Scary Places).* New York: Bearport (2008).

Learn More Online

To learn more about haunted caves, visit
www.bearportpublishing.com/ScaryPlaces

Index

About the Author

Natalie Lunis has written many nonfiction books for children. She lives in New York's lower Hudson River Valley—the home of the Headless Horseman.

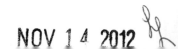